PIANO · VOCAL · GUITAR

THE EARLY 60s

FEATURING THE ROCK HITS: BARBARA ANN
· DUKE OF EARL · RUNAWAY · UNDER THE
BOARDWALK · WIPE OUT · AND MANY MORE
PLUS PHOTOS, A ROCK HISTORY AND GLOSSARY

COVER BACKGROUND: WESTLIGHT

ISBN #0-7935-0020-6

Hal Leonard Publishing Corporation
7777 West Bluemound Road P.O. Box 13819 Milwaukee, WI 53213

CHRONOLOGICAL CONTENTS

ALPHABETICAL CONTENTS

THE EARLY 60s

TO QUOTE A FAMILIAR LINE — "IT WAS THE BEST OF TIMES, IT WAS THE WORST OF TIMES." JOHN F. KENNEDY WAS ELECTED PRESIDENT. HE WAS YOUNG AND VITAL AND HE SYMBOLIZED A FRESH NEW START AND ATTITUDE IN THE COUNTRY. IT WAS A TIME WHEN THE COUNTRY'S YOUTH WERE GETTING READY TO TAKE HOLD OF AMERICA AND TO CHANGE IT. MUSIC WOULD BE ONE OF THE VEHICLES OF CHANGE. BUT FIRST, TEENS WOULD HAVE ONE LAST LIGHTHEARTED MUSICAL FLING AND DANCE THE NIGHT AWAY.

THE BRILL BUILDING

The dawning of the '60s also brought the dawning of the idea to the music business that rock and roll was here to stay. Rock was even old enough to have a song full of reminiscences in "Those Oldies But Goodies (Remind Me Of You)." The audience was maturing and the sound was beginning to be integrated into the catalogs of the Tin Pan Alley music publishers, just as the Alley was about to move uptown.

The newer music publishers were renting space uptown in the Brill building at 1619 Broadway. Their writers were already schooled in rock (they had cut their teeth on it), they had the influence of the great tunesmiths of Tin Pan Alley, and they had a "genuine empathy with teenagers—their values, interests, emotional needs and slang."* They also had the benefit of the most professional songpluggers in the business, the ones who knew the value of well-crafted music and lyric and could sell it to the major record companies right down the block. The Brill Building alumni were Carole King and Gerry Goffin, Barry Mann and Cynthia Weil, Bobby Darin, Neil Diamond, Howard Greenfield and Neil Sedaka, Burt Bacharach and Hal David, Doc Pomus and Mort Shuman, Jeff Barry and Ellie Greenwich, Bert Berns, Jerry Leiber and Mike Stoller (who were responsible for bringing Phil Spector to New York—making Spector an honorary Brill-ite).

*"The Rolling Stone History of Rock And Roll/'Brill Building' Chapter" by Greg Shaw

DO WAH DIDDY DIDDY - THE LAST GREAT DAYS OF DOO WOP

At the turn of the sixties, both New York (home of the *a cappella* street corner groups) and Phil Spector were responsible for spawning new doo wop sounds.

From across the river in New Jersey, the Varietones and Frankie Castelluccio became known as the Four Lovers with Frankie Valli. They had a minor hit in '56 on RCA and went back to the local club scene. After a gig in the Four Seasons Cocktail Lounge, located in a bowling alley, they became the Four Seasons. In '59, they became backup singers for veteran producer ("Silhouettes" by the Rays) Bob Crewe's Swan Records (first USA home of the Beatles).

When singer/songwriter Bob Gaudio joined the Four Seasons in 1960, he'd already penned chart hits, including "Short, Shorts" for the Royal Teens in 1958. Crewe, acting as the group's producer, helped mold their sound around Valli's signature falsetto and Gaudio's straightforward songs with distinctive hooks written specifically for the group's structure. Crewe got the group signed with Vee-Jay Records (also a short-lived label for the Beatles) and produced a string of huge hits. In 1962, their first hit "Sherry" introduced Valli's falsetto with the group singing tight harmonies in the background. It was followed in rapid succession by "Big Girls Don't Cry" and "Walk Like A Man." Over the next 20 years, their sales would total over 80 million units.

The only doo wop tune "Goin' Out Of My Head" to become a standard was also sung by the unique falsetto of Little Anthony. Brooklynite Anthony Gourdine got his nickname from DJ Alan Freed and already had had several

COURTESY OF RHINO RECORDS

chart hits when this was released. Anthony, with his group the Imperials, gave this tune the most emotional, spine-tingling interpretation and although it only went to six on the charts, it became an enduring hit. It was a hit again in 1968, sung by the Lettermen as part of a medley with "Can't Take My Eyes Off Of You" (which was a hit by Frankie Valli in 1967).

"Duke Of Earl" was a surprising hit from Gene Chandler, who was usually known as a consummate soul singer (and cohort of Curtis Mayfield, see *Soul*). His use of the title as the pounding background *doo wop* was equivalent to brain-washing – once heard, it could never be forgotten.

The "British Invasion" (see *History Of Rock – The Mid 60s*) in 1964 heralded an end to doo wop on the charts. Ironically, the last doo wop tune on the charts for a long while was by the British Group, Manfred Mann. Their simple, happy "Do Wah Diddy Diddy" was written by Brill-ites Jeff Barry and Ellie Greenwich. The group had strong rhythm and blues background, and most of their hits were written by American writers.

BIG GIRLS DON'T CRY — THE GIRL GROUPS AND PHIL SPECTOR

The girl groups came late into doo wop and hailed mostly from the New York area. Their popularity was aimed directly at the teen market. The subject matter was the giggling slumber party revelations with added sock hop beats, and the occasional back-seat-of-the-'57-Chevy sensuality of the late '50s and early '60s. Their boyfriends were the main focus of their songs, and whether he was "back" and ready to protect her, or made her heart stand still, or led the pack (or laundromat) or she finally got him to the chapel, the sound was clear, simple and enduring.

New Jerseyites, the Shirelles were the first girl-group to have a number one record and the first to have two recordings in the Top 10 simultaneously. Producer/arranger Luther Dixon developed their sound, balancing lead against background singing with great finesse and co-writing some of the tunes. However, most of the group's songs came directly from the stalwarts of the Brill Building such as Carole King. Their tune "Soldier Boy" is most typical of the girl group subject matter of the early '60s.

Another typical lyric came from the Angels, also from New Jersey, in their song "My Boyfriend's Back" with its intro narrative and the pre-women's lib stance of having their boyfriend protect them. They were the first white girl rock group to have a number one record.

Although the Dixie Cups came from New Orleans, they were on Leiber and Stoller's (see *THE BRILL BUILDING* and *History Of Rock – The Birth Of Rock & Roll*) Red Bird record label, one that primarily recorded girl groups. Ellie Greenwich, Jeff Barry and Phil Spector wrote the group's biggest hit "Chapel Of Love," a simple ditty with plain doo-wopping in the background that struck a responsive chord in a huge generation of post-teen, soon-to-be-married adults.

Red Bird's Shangri-Las were rock's first tough girls; their songs were much more brazen than their doo-wopping sisters' of the time. For them, the uniform was the black-denim-trousers-motorcycle-boots of raunchy rock. Their sound had an eerie detached feeling and their songs were often broken up with narrative and sound effects. "Leader Of The Pack," another Ellie Greenwich/Jeff Barry tune (see *THE BRILL BUILDING*) produced by Shadow Morton was their biggest hit. It was a real rebellious-teen song, where the parents don't approve of the daughter's motorcycle-riding boyfriend. He speeds off into the sunset in a huff and dies in a crash of glory (gory). (Strangely, there were many "grief" songs in the early '60s, such as Ray Peterson's "Tell Laura I Love Her" where a guy dies in a race trying to earn enough money to buy his girlfriend a ring.)

The smooth and delightful Crystals were produced by Phil Spector and their songs were fine illustrations of his "wall of sound." Their number 1 hit, "He's A Rebel," a song about a rebel who nonetheless treated his girlfriend well, was written by Gene Pitney (see *THE HEARTBREAKERS*). Spector added layers of instrumentation to its production and outside singers Darlene Love and her group the Blossoms. Love's voice was so versatile, that Spector added her talents to several other groups he produced.

Spector came out of New York, the epitome of a '50s lost teen, then he "reinvented" himself with pure energy. Moving to Los Angeles, he wrote the song, "To Know Him Is To Love Him," based on his father's epitaph and produced a hit with the Teddy Bears. He then went to Philadelphia at the height of the *Bandstand* years and produced more records. On to New York, where he hung around the Brill Building and talked Atlantic Records into letting him produce some sides. One of the recordings was Ben E. King's "Spanish Harlem," which he co-wrote with Jerry Leiber. When the royalties came in, he established his own label, Philles (Phil-Les formed originally with publishing industry giant Lester Sill). At Philles, he produced the Crystals, Bob B. Soxx and the Blue Jeans and the Ronettes. The song concepts were pure teen romance and rebellion. His "wall of sound" came from the then new practice of multitracking and overdubbing, and gave rock its deepest, fullest, most polished sound to date.

All of this happened *before* Spector was 21 years old. Phil Spector's production prowess and contributions to rock go deep and high, he produced hits well into the '70s (some with the individual Beatles), but many deem the early '60s as his most productive years.

SURFIN' U.S.A.

The first surfing tunes were instrumentals and it was Dick Dale who, though not heard much beyond Southern California, was credited with the distillation of the surfing sound. He recorded high-energy instrumental music using a reverb unit from Leo Fender (the developer of the Telecaster and Stratocaster guitars and Fender Bass) that gave the guitar a whole new rough echoey sound.

"Pipeline" and "Wipe Out" were the biggest and best surfing instrumentals recorded. "Pipeline" was named after the most challenging surfing spot in Hawaii. The Chantay's introductory plunging bass line in the song is said to be the sound equivalent of riding a twenty foot Pipeline wave.

EYEWITNESS ACCOUNT • Richard Delvy: "Wipe Out," the surfing term for being knocked off the board by a wave, was initially the homegrown product of the Surfaris. They made the single to promote themselves while still a Southern California high school band. Richard Delvy of the Challengers (another surf group of superb musicianship who *covered*

THE CHALLENGERS: ED FOURNIER, RANDY NUART, RICHARD DELVY, ART FISHER, PHIL PRUDEN. (COURTESY OF RICHARD DELVY)

most of the major surfing hits) was hipped to the group by a local record distributor, obtained the rights, and then released the recording on his own Princess label. It was originally the B side, but the response to its novel and driving sound pushed it right to number 2 on the charts. Strangely, the Surfaris didn't turn up for their Lp recording session, so only two cuts are by them, the rest are by the Challengers. (Delvy went on to be musical director of *Hollywood A Go Go*, a popular music TV show in the '60s, and continues to be a successful music producer and publisher today.)

The Beach Boys became the paramount surfing group. Hailing from Hawthorne, a beach community abutting Los Angeles, the brothers, Brian, Dennis and Carl Wilson, cousin Mike Love and friend Al Jardine released their first single, "Surfin'," in 1962 on the tiny Candix label. Brian was prone to writing hot rod tunes; Dennis was the surfer in the group and it was he who suggested the surfing theme to Dennis and Mike Love. When Capitol Records released the Beach Boys next single, they made a hot rod song "409" the A side and "Surfin' Safari" the B side. However, "Surfin' Safari" received all the attention and went up to fourteen on the charts.

This still didn't reassure Capitol as to the national appeal of surf music, so they released the tune "Ten Little Indians," which went nowhere. Finally, Capitol tried the magic formula again and released "Surfin' U.S.A." backed with a hot-rod song, "Shut Down," followed by "Surfer Girl" backed with car song, "Little Deuce Coupe." These tunes went to #3 and #7 respectively on the charts, assuring Capitol that an "endless summer" did have broad appeal.

The Beach Boys made surfing such a national phenomenon that the surfing jargon was heard in oceanless places such as New Hampshire and Montana and surfboards and surfing accouterments were being shipped to the flatlands of the Midwest. Hollywood even jumped on the bandwagon with their spate of *Beach-Blanket-Bikini* movies starring the grown-up '50s' idols Frankie Avalon and Annette Funicello.

The Beach Boys' trademark was their fresh California sound with clean, clear harmonies reminiscent of mid-'50s middle-of-the-road groups with the rauchy seasoning of a Chuck Berry rhythm and riff or two (an inkling of Berry's wide influence on rock and guitar). Brian Wilson, who wrote most of the songs, showed himself to be a fine musician, writer and producer. And as time went on (and his audience matured), he showed a more complex and serious side to his talent. He became one of the first songwriter/musician/producer/leaders in the business, making the Beach Boys one of the first self-produced groups. The multiple pressures of stardom caught up with Brian in 1964 when he suffered a nervous breakdown and confined his musical activities to writing and producing (his best tunes were yet to come).

The Beach Boys had had just one hit when they backed up the already seasoned professionals Jan Berry and Dean Torrence at an L.A. dance. Jan and Dean had the surfer's look—tan, sleek, clean cut, great smiles. So when their manager, Lou Adler,* suggested they might record a surfing song, the duo recalled that they were impressed with Brian Wilson's writing. Wilson responded with the partially written "Surf City," which he and Jan completed. It became the duo's biggest hit.

The give-and-take between the Beach Boys and Jan and Dean was unique in rock annals of that day (not until the late '80s was it to happen again). They wrote together and sang back-up on each others' records (uncredited). Jan and Dean had ten hits from '63 to '66, when Jan was horribly injured and paralyzed in an automobile accident. Dean went on to be a marvelous graphic artist, designing many memorable record covers. Amazingly, Jan recovered to the point that they were able to perform again by the late '70s.

*Producer/manager Adler went on to considerable fame himself (see *History Of Rock – The Mid '60s* and *History Of Rock – The Late '60s*).

JAN AND DEAN (COURTESY OF DEAN TORRENCE)

SAVE THE LAST DANCE FOR ME — WELL THEN, LET'S TWIST AGAIN

The early '60s was a time ripe for new dances. The bop had been the mainstay of rock dancing for almost four years and the pervasive Latin rhythms in the late '50s had everyone doing a variety of Latin dances, but those were more for *adults*. Songs and the dances that they spawned such as "Monster Mash" (for the mashed potato) by Bobby Pickett and The Crypt-Kickers, "Bristol Stomp" by the Dovells and "The Wah Watusi" by the Orlons were relatively short-lived. Many of these recordings came out of Philadelphia's Cameo Records, which had an unerring instinct for hits in the late '50s and early '60s. The dances, in retrospect, seem silly, but then the early '60s were initially a light-hearted time, especially for teens.

However, "The Twist," the dance that made the covers of *Time* and *Newsweek*, owes it popularity to the best teen media network of all time, *American Bandstand*. R & B mainstay Hank Ballard wrote and recorded "The Twist" in '59 after having two hits, "Kansas City" and "Finger Poppin' Time." It became an R & B chart hit and sparked a new dance in the Black communities. In the summer of '60, Dick Clark spotted a couple doing it on his show (he said the gyrations "resembled something a bellydancer did to climax her performance") and was a bit wary to have it on-screen. Within a week, however, the dance had spread to all the "regulars" (see *History Of Rock – The Late '50s*). Clark notified a friend, Bernie Lowe, at Cameo Records of this growing trend, and Lowe recorded the tune with a new artist Ernest Evans a.k.a. Chubby Checker.

Checker had been working as a chicken plucker and singing while he worked. His boss connected him with Lowe at Cameo who gave him his first break by cutting a novelty Christmas record for the Bandstand. Cameo promoted "The Twist" to the hilt. Checker was all personality and appeal and had all the right moves for the dance.

Not only did "The Twist" top the charts in the fall of '60, but it also topped the charts in January of 1962 and, in between, Checker had a hit with "Let's Twist Again." There were legions of twist songs, the most famous being the Isley Brothers' "Twist And Shout" and "The Peppermint Twist" by Joey Dee and His Starliters, who were the house band at a New York club, the Peppermint Lounge. Instrumentalist Dee sang lead on the record when the singer hired to sing lead couldn't get the right "feel."

The Peppermint Lounge became very popular when Atlantic Records' head, Ahmet Ertegun, brought all of his very trendy friends (including Jackie Kennedy) there to twist and the press got wind of it. The publicity was so fabulous that it gave the dance another resurgence of popularity.

When Tex-Mex meets rock and roll meets Lawrence of Arabia, what do you have? *An apt description of Sam the Sham and the Pharaohs.* Domingo Samudio (Sam) and his group capitalized on the costumey fad that prevailed amongst rock groups by wearing turbans and robes. Their rhythmic, infectious, Tex-Mex sound, especially on "Wooly Bully," was perfect for dancing. Samudio used the electronic organ with some of its novelty sounds to good effect; a trend that would continue and expand eventually into synthesis.

SOUL TO ROCK AND ROLL

The Drifters were aptly named, in the course of their history they've had over fifty members and lasted for almost thirty years. Their first era from 1953 to 1958 produced a string of R & B hits with occasional crossover to the pop charts. The kingpin of the group was the singer Clyde McPhatter who quit the group in '58 for a solo career and precipitated the group's breakup. The manager, George Treadwell, then shifted another of his groups, the Five Crowns and singer Ben E. King and dubbed them the Drifters.

Signed to Atlantic Records and produced originally by Ahmet Ertegun and Jerry Wexler, the new lineup of the Drifters was produced by Leiber and Stoller who added a pop sound to the rhythm and blues and gospel undertones, including adding strings. This combination paid off with many hits on the pop charts. "Save The Last Dance For Me" was their biggest of all and a tune that's been covered numerous times since. Ben E. King left the group just after this hit, but Rudy Lewis assumed the lead singer duties adroitly and the hits, including "Under The Boardwalk," continued through the mid-'60s.

Many were sure that King was foolish to leave the Drifters, but a year later he hit the charts with Jerry Leiber and Phil Spector's "Spanish Harlem," followed immediately by a tune he cowrote, "Stand By Me." He had other hits in the early '60s, one in the '70s and then "Stand By Me" came back in 1986 as a film title theme and the song was a hit again!

Jerry Butler was a mover and shaper of the Chicago brand of R & B and soul (see *History Of Rock – The Late '50s*). Initially he sang with Curtis Mayfield in the Impressions, but when the group didn't have a hit after their first in 1958, Butler split for a solo career. He did, however, continue his association with Mayfield, and together they wrote "He Will Break Your Heart." Butler had a smooth delivery and crossed over into the pop and eventually the MOR charts.

Brook Benton had a long stream of hits from 1959 through 1964 (and then again in 1970). He wrote many of his hits, and his duo "Baby (You've Got What It Takes)" with Dinah Washington clearly showed his part blues, part gospel stylization. Several others of his hits were covers of old R & B standards with a rock tinge.

Jimmy Reed's bluesy "Bright Lights, Big City" only made it to #58 on the charts, but it became an R & B standard. This singer/songwriter/guitarist/harmonica player was known for his delta blues style of guitar and powerful delivery. He had fourteen chart hits and a slew of covers of his tunes by such rock superstars as Aretha Franklin and Little Richard. Many English bands of the mid-'60s, most notably The Rolling Stones, the Animals and the Who reported that his sound was highly influential on their music.

Many of soul's greatest acts were brought to the public's attention via Atlantic Records and the astute ears of Ahmet Ertegun and Jerry Wexler. Ertegun was the son of the Turkish ambassador to the U.S. When their father died, Ahmet and his brother Nesuhi decided not to return to Turkey, but to stay in the U.S. and become involved in the music business. In the late '40s, in order to raise money to start their record company they auctioned off their huge record collection of 25,000 jazz and blues recordings (78 rpms). Wexler came to them by way of BMI and Billboard Magazine (where he was responsible for changing the name of "Race Music" charts to "Rhythm and Blues" charts).

RAY CHARLES (COURTESY OF RAY CHARLES PRODUCTIONS)

By the mid-'50s, Atlantic was one of the top R & B labels, and by combining R & B with pop, they soon became a rock and soul label as well. They signed and developed Joe Turner, Ruth Brown, the Coasters, the Drifters, Ben E. King, Cyde McPhatter, Ray Charles and Aretha Franklin. (Later they would sign the Rolling Stones and Crosby, Stills, Nash & Young.) They continue to be a major force in the music business.

"Hit The Road Jack" was the eighth foray on the charts for Ray Charles, "The Father Of Soul" (see *History Of Rock – The Late '50s*). It was an unusual song for Charles—a lightly orchestrated, medium tempo, finger-snapping kind of tune. But then, Charles' styles ranged from blues to gospel, from swing to jazz, from country to pop; one really couldn't categorize him. Charles described soul music as "...when you take a song and make it a part of you—a part that's so true and so real that people think it must have happened to you. I'm not satisfied unless I can make them feel what I feel."

Meanwhile in the early '60s in Detroit, Berry Gordy was bringing about another change in soul as he was molding the slickest packages of black music talent and developing Motown Records in Detroit (see *History Of Rock – The Mid '60s*). Blues, R & B and soul became America's most powerful musical influences on the world's upcoming artists.

BERRY GORDY (COURTESY OF MCA RECORDS)

PUT ON YOUR HI-HEEL SNEAKERS

It never fails, in every era there are novelty tunes and the early '60s were no exception. It wasn't always easy to break them, even if their subject matter was the most *au courant* fashion or TV fad.

EYEWITNESS ACCOUNT • Irwin Pincus: Songwriters Lee Pockriss and Paul Vance sat down at the piano in the New York office of successful publisher Gil Pincus ("Come Go With Me," "Old Cape Cod") and played their latest creation "Itsy Bitsy Teenie Weenie Yellow Polkadot Bikini" for Gil and his son Irwin. Gil thought the tune could be a hit, but it was up to Irwin to go out (songplug) and find someone to record it. "I played it for everyone for a year and a half at all the record companies; they laughed me out their doors," recounts Irwin.

"Finally, I took the song to Dick Wolf, head of A & R at Kapp Records and he loved it! But I wasn't happy when he told me he was going to put it out with an unknown singer, Brian Hyland. However, Kapp did put ace record promotion man, Irwin Zucker onto Hyland's recording. Early on a Friday morning, Zucker hit every radio station in L.A. and by that very evening he called me to tell me the song was a hit. By Monday, it was playing all over the country [just in time for summer and the latest bathing suit fad], it was a hit within a week." (Hyland went on to have several chart hits, showing himself to have a truly lovely voice with a haunting quality. Zucker is now equally successful as a book publicist in L.A.)

One of the two groups that the Pacific Northwest spawned in the early '60s were the Kingsmen (the others were the Ventures). Their version of songwriter Richard Berry's "Louie, Louie" became a classic rock tune, which was covered many times over. (In fact, a recording of eleven different versions of "Louie, Louie," inlcuding a marching band version, was released in the mid-'80s.) Their third and last hit was "Jolly Green Giant," which no doubt grew out of the frozen foods' character who was then currently "ho-ho-ho-ing" his way through TV commercials. (By the way, it was the Kingsmen-type of band that later spawned the name "garage" band which led to punk rock and other sounds in the '80s.)

Another rock classic "Hi Heel Sneakers" paid homage once more to a clothing fad, while adding a bit of the absurd. But the song worked well enough to become a hit all over again by Jose Feliciano in the late '60s. The comic strip character "Alley-Oop" even had a silly song on the charts, which was redeemed somewhat because of its good strong dance beat.

ONLY LOVE CAN BREAK A HEART – THE HEARTBREAKERS

This was an era where many rock singers really had "pipes," voices that could send chills through you or had a delivery and style that played on one's emotions. Gene Pitney's soaring recording of "Only Love Can Break A Heart" was a dramatic example of the rock ballad singer. A consummate musician and songwriter, Pitney wrote Rick Nelson's "Hello Mary Lou" and the Crystals "He's A Rebel." Oddly, he relied on the budding team of Burt Bacharach and Hal David for his hits.

EYEWITNESS ACCOUNT •Bernie Wayne: By 1962, Bobby Vinton had had a couple hits that had colors in their titles, "Roses Are Red (My Love)" and "Blue On Blue," plus several smooth rock/ballad chart ticklers. He hit his stride with "Blue Velvet," an absolutely intense version that still makes people stop and listen whenever it's played.

Songwriter Bernie Wayne (who also wrote "[Here She Comes] Miss America") relates that in 1953 while visiting Richmond, Virginia he met a beautiful lady wearing blue velvet and wrote the song. He felt, however, it was a strange song for this era of early rock and sappy pop. Wayne took to veteran A & R man, Mitch Miller at Columbia Records and sang just the first line when Miller stopped him and said, "Who do you want to sing it – Tony Bennett or Frank Sinatra?" Wayne picked Tony Bennett who recorded the song just two days later.

Ten years later while dining in Lindy's in New York, Wayne was astonished to hear Bobby Vinton's version on the sound system and to discover it was zooming up the charts to #1. He called Vinton, who told him that he had heard Tony Bennett's "Blue Velvet" when he was a kid and promised himself someday he would record it. (In 1986 at the premiere of the movie *Blue Velvet,* director David Lynch told Wayne that when he heard Bobby Vinton's "Blue Velvet" in 1963, it became his favorite song and he vowed that someday he'd use it in a movie.)

By 1960, Dion and The Belmonts were firmly entrenched in pop music (see *History of Rock – The Late '50s*). They came out of the sidewalk doo-wop tradition of the Bronx and their songs had a good grasp of teen emotions and lingo. When one of the group members was drafted in 1960, Dion [Di Mucci] decided to pursue a solo career. His sound was tougher and sexier than some of the other teen idols and his audience was wider. Three of his tunes from the early '60s became rock classics—"Runaround Sue," "The Wanderer," and "Ruby Baby" — but the British Invasion and a bout with drugs cut into his productivity until his milestone recording in 1968 of "Abraham, Martin and John" (see *History of Rock – The Late '60s*).

As the youngest member of television's first family on *The Adventures of Ozzie And Harriet,*

Ricky Nelson had a ready-made following and a squeaky clean image, even with his moody sex appeal. That image made him "safer" than Elvis, i.e. more acceptable to parents, but ironically it was Presley who had the biggest musical influence on Nelson. So, Nelson played and sang in an urban rockabilly style as was the sound on "Hello Mary Lou." Some of his earlier hits were by rockabilly singer/songwriters Dorsey and Johnny Burnette and his band consisted of consummate rock musicians including James Burton, one of rockabilly's most brilliant guitarists (who would later play with Presley, and who while working with Nelson also "invented" super-light gauge strings by putting banjo strings on his Telecaster to make it easier to bend notes). Nelson's recordings that followed were covers of standards with one last major hit, "Garden Party," in 1972. He died in an airplane crash on the way to a concert. His children have continued the family show business tradition.

PLAY ME SOME OF THAT ROCK AND ROLL MUSIC

It was inevitable that as rock came into its own as a musical form that it would develop and become more complex. Every trend added to the intricacy of the sound—Latin rock, rockabilly, calypso and the basis of rock, rhythm and blues, and developments in electronics.

The early '60s were at the edge of what was to become the age of the guitar. In 1952, Gibson introduced the Les Paul electric solid bodies and in 1953 Fender produced the "work horse" of rock, the Stratocaster. By 1957, the humbucking pickup gave a wonderfully gutsy sound to solid-body guitars. The '50s and early '60s also ushered in the usage of stereo wiring, twin-neck guitars, semi-solid guitars, plus more versatile control circuitry to sustain and control feedback and to service high-energy rock music. The move in the early '60s was from pure, clean sound to controlled distortion with devices such as the wah-wah pedal, the fuzz-box, univibe and octave divider.

The Ventures came out of the Pacific Northwest scene that favored instrumental rock. They were guitar-oriented group with a clean, straight-ahead rock sound marked by heavy use of the tremolo arm effect. Their influences were Chet Atkins and Les Paul and it was Atkins' version of Johnny Smith's "Walk Don't Run" that introduced the group to what was to become a hit for them twice, in 1960 and 1964. The Ventures had several instrumental hits of standards and rock tunes and capitalized on the instrumental surfing craze as well, but oddly for a rock group they were known for their sales of albums (unique in this era). They were also notable for their recording sessions which featured such luminaries as Leon Russell, David Gates and Glen Campbell.

Chuck Berry is the most influential guitarist of early rock. Almost every rock guitarist in every genre credits him with some sort of influence on their playing. His songs were anthems of teenage life and, as with his music, he articulated them clearly to ensure that his audience understood every nuance.

Born in San Jose, California, Berry's family moved to St. Louis in the '30s where Berry's music experiences came from school glee clubs and church choirs. He worked as a hairdresser and in a car factory, and performed with a three-piece blues group in the evenings and on weekends.

In 1955, he did a demo recording and took it to seminal bluesman Muddy Waters in Chicago. Waters linked Berry up with Leonard Chess of Chess Records. Chess liked an early version of "Maybellene" entitled "Ida Red," but made Berry clean it up considerably for radio play. The polished version (blues great Willie Dixon was on the session) hit the R & B charts in 1955 and with the help of Alan Freed (see *History Of Rock – The Birth Of Rock & Roll*) crossed over to the pop charts as did nine tunes in the '50s. Berry's next roll of hits started all over in the mid-'60s and continued sporadically, but unabated.

Berry was such a flamboyant showman that his famous "duckwalk" (playing and hopping around the stage in a squat) was captured in several classic rock films including

Go, Johnny, Go and *Rock, Rock, Rock* in the '50s (and a documentary with Rolling Stone Keith Richard in the '80s). He was the first person to be elected to the Rock Music Hall Of Fame. But most important were his guitar *chops*. That amalgam of rhythm and blues beat and chords with country runs and straight-ahead electric guitar amplification introduced riffs and techniques that molded rock guitar forever.

Keyboards took a backseat in the early '60s recordings, but there were some highlights such as Del Shannon's recording of "Runaway" with its unique sound on an electric organ called a Musitron.

LET ME TELL YOU 'BOUT THE BIRDS AND THE BEES...

For the most part, early '60s rock did not strive for that sense of freedom that was more typical of early rock and rhythm and blues. Even songs that had "rebellion"-type lyric were almost formula in their appeal to adolescent-dreams and desires. Increasingly, however, attention was being paid to production values and total sound (Shadow Morton, Phil Spector, Brian Wilson) as well as more exciting and wilder instrumental experimentation.

On another side of music, the folk music scene was burgeoning. It had been a strong underground element in the '50s in response to the very repressive governmental attitudes and prevailing bigotry in the country. Folk music was beginning to gain favor with the masses as its messages for civil rights, ecology and disarmament (we thought) were seemingly those of the current Kennedy administration. Woody Guthrie, Leadbelly, Pete Seeger, the Journeymen and the Kingston Trio laid the groundwork (and contributed some of the musicians) for the next era of folk rock when Peter, Paul and Mary, Joan Baez and Bob Dylan would be the purveyors of the songs of social significance. Their songs would echo forth following John Kennedy's assassination. An age of innocence was lost.

The most powerful teen generation ever suddenly came of age in late 1963. They were part of the civil rights marches on Washington, hearing Martin Luther King, Jr. saying "I have a dream." They had more sexual freedom, courtesy of the "pill." They lauded the new laws banning sex discrimination and heartily supported the nuclear test ban on atmospheric, underwater and outer space testing signed by the U.S., Russia and Great Britain. It was a generation whose voice was heard and carried with music, and who was about to make their music change the world. ■

ROCK AND ROLL GLOSSARY – THE EARLY '60S

acid rock: Highly amplified music with distorted electronic effects; term coined in late '60s because of the use of acid (LSD) by many artists. Forerunner of heavy metal.

AOR: *Album-Oriented-Rock* – a chart term for album cut airplay on certain broad spectrum FM radio stations.

artists and repertoire: The record company personnel responsible for talent acquisition, overseeing their production (and repertoire) and their activities.

ax: A musical instrument.

blast: Having a good time.

bop: n. The bop, a dance, a take off of the swing from the '40s. **v.** To bop, to dance; to go out.

Brill Building: Located at 1619 Broadway in New York City. Home of hundreds of music publishers' offices. Many, many hits were born there.

bugged: To be bothered.

busted: Arrested.

C&W: Country and western music.

chart: A sequential list of hits; a *written down* musical arrangement (improvised arrangement is called a *head* arrangement).

chops: A musician's playing technique, ability.

cool: In the '50s, to be *hip*, in style, okay.

cover: A new recording of a previously recorded song. A common practice in the '50s was for white artists to cover hits by black R&B artists.

crossover: Songs that "cross over" from one chart to another, such as from a country chart to a pop chart.

cut: n. A record; or one song on an album. **v.** To make (cut) a recording.

demo: A demonstration record; used by songwriters and publishers to sell their songs to artists.

dig: To understand, i.e. "Do you dig it?" Late '50s.

disco: Dance club, from the French *discotèque;* a mid '60s fad.

distortion devices: For guitar — *wah-wah pedal, fuzz tone, reverb, echo, tremolo.*

doo wop: A type of close harmony singing, usually with sparse instrumental accompaniment, unique in the use of nonsense syllables as rhythmic background or "punctuation."

dub: n. A copy of the *master*. **v.** To record from a *master;* to insert a new sound, or synchronize one sound with another sound (overdub).

far out: Wonderful, great, terrific!

feedback: On a guitar set for feedback, a string will vibrate at a certain pitch so that the sound is picked up by the amplifier and fed back into the string to increase its vibration at that pitch.

flipped out: To really like something/ someone, '50s.

flaked out: Tired.

funk/funky: A rhythm and blues sound, usually lowdown, rhythmic and rough.

fuzztone: A device on a guitar that changes the shape of the soundwave so that the music from the amplifier has a blurred or fuzzy sound. First used by Link Wray.

groove: n. Where music really "clicks" and comes together for the listener, especially rhythmically; as in "in the groove." **v.** To *groove* is to enjoy, be one with (the music or one's lover).

grounded: Not permitted by parents to drive the car or go out.

gung ho: Enthusiastic.

head: Someone who takes drugs.

heavy: Serious.

hip: Cool, with it, late '50s.

hook: A repetitive phrase, usually in the chorus, that catches the listener's attention.

hot-doggers: Surfers, early '60s.

jive: n. Slang or colloquial expressions derived from blues slang, used first in the jazz sector and then in '50s rock.

licks: Short, melodic musical phrases which sometimes became musical "signatures" for artists.

master: n. Final, completed recording from which copies can be made. **v.** To *master;* to make a master.

mix: To balance all the tracks of a multitrack *master* to bring it to final product status.

MOR: *Middle Of The Road* – a chart term for music, usually ballads, that bridged the gap between easy listening and rock.

nitty gritty: Getting to the soul of something, early '60s.

overdub: To add parts to and synchronize them in a multitrack recording.

put down: A criticism.

put-on: n. A lie. **v.** Lead someone on.

R&B: *Rhythm & blues;* post World War II black music, replacing the previous appellation of "race" music.

reverb: On guitar, an echo-like sound effect.

riff: A pattern of music, sometimes repetitive; usually played by a rhythm instrument — guitar, bass, drum or keyboards.

rumble: A fight, late '50s.

scene: Where it's happening, late '50s.

shook up: Upset, late '50s.

shot down: Rejected, early '60s.

square: Unhip, uncool, conservative, unknowing in the ways of rock and roll; usually pertaining to one's parents.

standard: A song that continues to remain popular and receive many *covers* over the years.

stiff: n. A recording that doesn't make it. **v.** to cheat someone.

stoned: High on drugs.

studio musician: A free-lance musician who works primarily in recording studios.

swing: Late '50s, to belong.

turn on: n. A *turn-on* – something interesting. **v.** To be *turned on* – to be sexually aroused, or on drugs.

turf: Territory, late '50s.

wah-wah pedal: On guitar, a device that distorts the sound by use of electric currents that vibrate the speakers to emphasize or de-emphasize the middle range of the sound output.

wheels: Car or any motorized transportation.

zonked: High (on drugs or alcohol), early '60s.

BABY
(YOU'VE GOT WHAT IT TAKES)

Words and Music by CLYDE OTIS
and MURRAY STEIN

Well, now it takes more____ than a rob - in

to make the win - ter go;____ And it takes two lips of fire____ to

melt a - way the snow.____ Well, it takes two hearts a - cook - in' to

16

ALLEY-OOP

Lively

By DALLAS FRAZIER

TELL LAURA I LOVE HER

Words and Music by JEFF BARRY
and BEN RALEIGH

WALK DON'T RUN

Words and Music by
JOHNNY SMITH

THE TWIST

Words and Music by
HANK BALLARD

SAVE THE LAST DANCE FOR ME

Words and Music by DOC POMUS
and MORT SHUMAN

HE WILL BREAK YOUR HEART

(A/K/A HE DON'T LOVE YOU)

By JERRY BUTLER,
CURTIS MAYFIELD, CALVIN CARTER

ITSY BITSY TEENIE WEENIE YELLOW POLKADOT BIKINI

Words and Music by PAUL J. VANCE
and LEE POCKRISS

Brightly, with humor

She was a-fraid to come out of the lock-er, She was as ner-vous as she___ could be; She was a-fraid to come out of the lock-er, She was a-fraid that some bod-y would see. (Two, three, four, Tell the peo-ple what she wore.) It was an It-sy Bit-sy Tee-nie Wee-nie Yel-low Pol-ka-dot Bi-ki-ni,

RUNAWAY

Moderately bright

Words and Music by DEL SHANNON
and MAX CROOK

As I walk a-long___ I won-der what went wrong___ with our love, a love that was___ so strong.

And as I still walk on___ I think of the things we've done___ to-

APACHE

Words and Music by
JERRY LORDAN

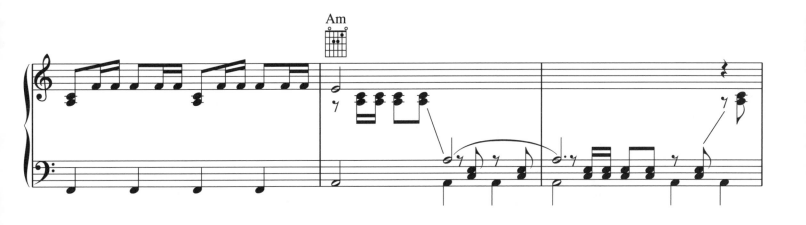

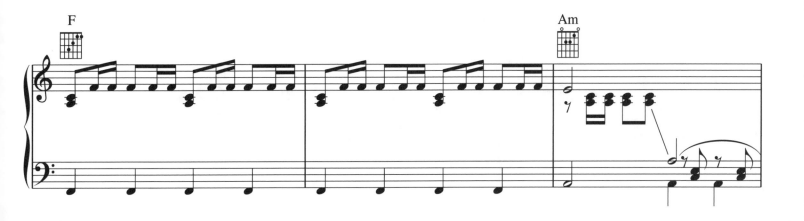

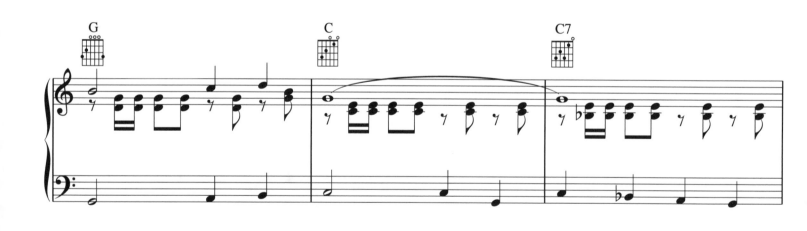

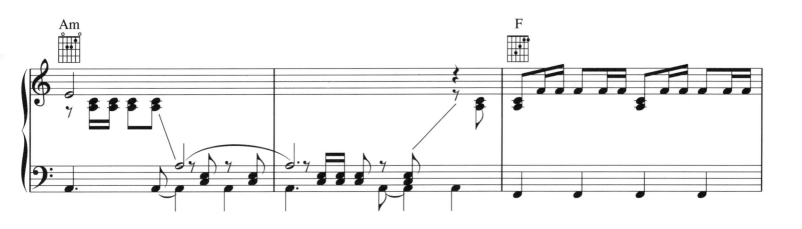

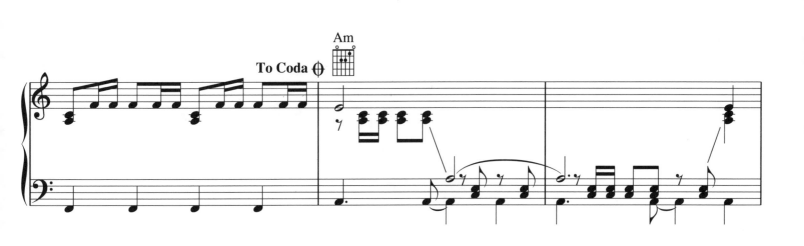

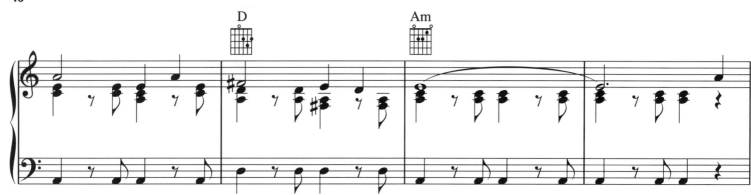

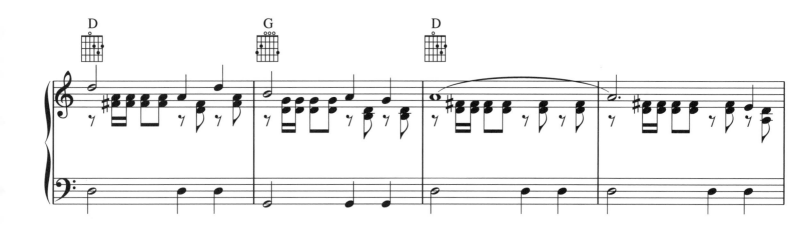

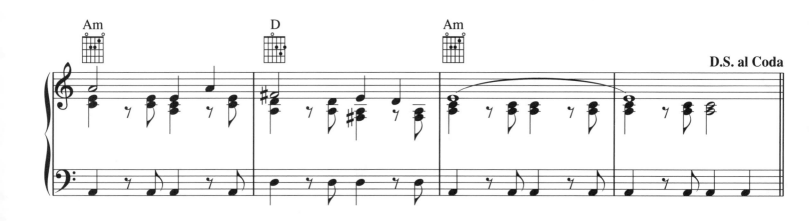

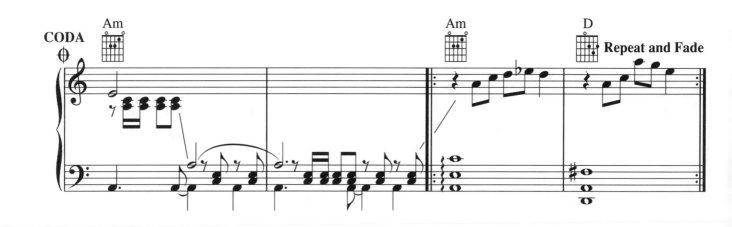

STAND BY ME

Words and Music by BEN E. KING,
JERRY LIEBER and MIKE STOLLER

HELLO MARY LOU
(GOODBYE HEART)

Words and Music by GENE PITNEY
and C. MANGIARACINA

BARBARA ANN

Words and Music by
FRED FASSERT

Bright Rock Tempo

THOSE OLDIES BUT GOODIES
(REMIND ME OF YOU)

Words and Music by PAUL POLITI
and NICK CURINGA

I LIKE IT LIKE THAT

Words and Music by KRIS KENNER
and ALLEN TOUSSAINT

LET'S TWIST AGAIN

Words by KAL MANN
Music by DAVE APPELL and KAL MANN

BRISTOL STOMP

Words and Music by KAL MANN
and DAVE APPELL

64

HIT THE ROAD JACK

Words and Music by
PERCY MAYFIELD

BRIGHT LIGHTS, BIG CITY

Words and Music by
JIMMY REED

WAH WATUSI

Words and Music by KAL MANN
and DAVE APPELL

74

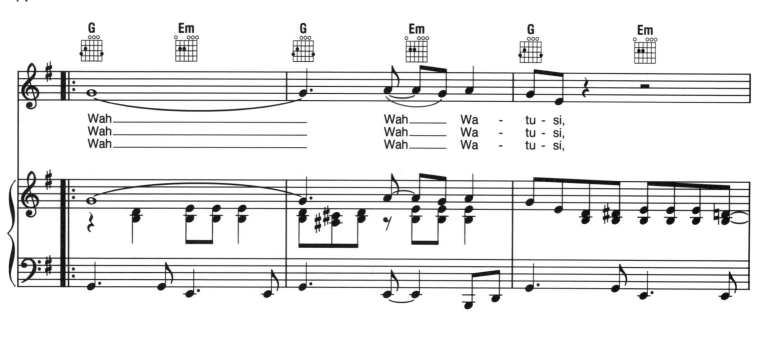

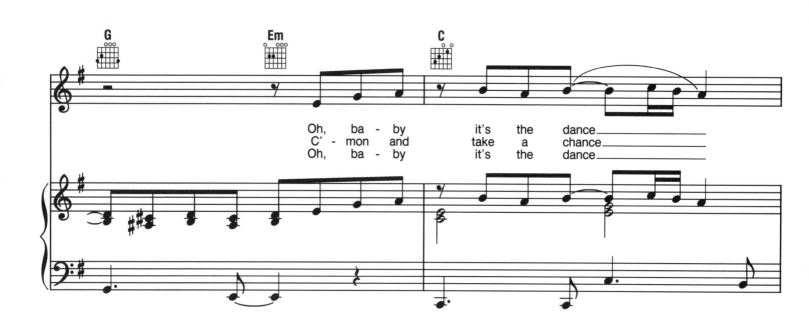

PEPPERMINT TWIST – PART I

Words and Music by JOEY DEE
and HENRY GLOVER

DUKE OF EARL

Moderately with a rock beat

Words and Music by EARL EDWARDS,
EUGENE DIXON and BERNICE WILLIAMS

As I walk through this world,
No - thing can stop the the
You will be the the

When I hold you,

Duke of Earl, And you are my girl, And
Duch - ess of Earl, When I walk through my Duke - dom, The

no one can hurt you, Yes I'm
par - a - dise we will share, I'm

PALISADES PARK

Words and Music by
CHUCK BARRIS

BREAKING UP IS HARD TO DO

Words and Music by NEIL SEDAKA
and HOWARD GREENFIELD

THINGS

Words and Music by
BOBBY DARIN

Ev-'ry night I sit here by my win- dow _ (win- dow.) _
Mem- o- ries are all I have to cling to _ (cling to) _ And

Star- ing at the lone- ly av- e- nue, (av- e- nue,) _
heart- aches are the friends I'm talk- ing to (talk- ing to.) _ When

Watch- ing lov- ers hold- ing hands and laugh- ing _ (laugh- ing) _ And
I'm not think- in' of a- just how much I love you, _ (love you,) _ Well, I'm

MONSTER MASH

Words and Music by BOBBY PICKETT
and LEONARD CAPIZZI

Medium Rock Beat

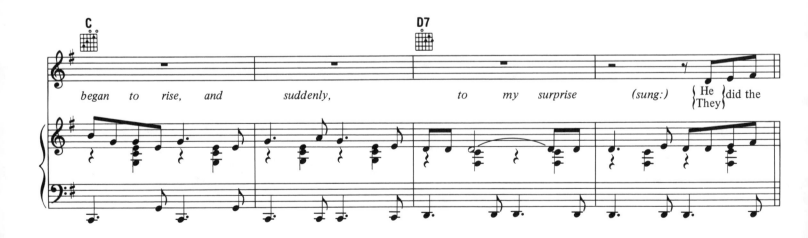

mash, *He did the monster mash.* The mon-ster mash. *It was a graveyard smash.* {He / They} did the

mash; *It caught on in a flash.* He did the mash. *He did the monster mash.* 2. From my *monster mash.*

Spoken: Mash good, easy, Igor, you impetuous young boy. Uh-uh-uh-uh.

Repeat and Fade

2. From my laboratory in the castle east.
To the master bedroom where the vampires feast.
The ghouls all came from their humble abodes
To catch a jolt from my electrodes.
(to Chorus: They did the mash)

3. The zombies were having fun,
The party had just begun.
The guests included Wolf-man,
Dracula, and his son.

4. The scene was rockin'; all were digging the sounds,
Igor on chains, backed by his baying hounds.
The coffin-bangers were about to arrive
With their vocal group "The Crypt-Kicker Five"
(to Chorus: They played the mash)

5. Out from his coffin, Drac's voice did ring;
Seems he was troubled by just one thing.
He opened the lid and shook his fist,
And said, "Whatever happened to my Transylvanian twist?"
(to Chorus: It's now the mash)

6. Now everything's cool, Drac's a part of the band
And my monster mash is the hit of the land.
For you, the living, this mash was meant too,
When you get to my door, tell them Boris sent you. *(till fade)*
(to Chorus: And you can mash)

SHERRY

Words and Music by
BOB GAUDIO

SURFIN' SAFARI

Words and Music by BRIAN WILSON
and MIKE LOVE

ONLY LOVE CAN BREAK A HEART

Words and Music by BURT BACHARACH
and HAL DAVID

BIG GIRLS DON'T CRY

Words and Music by BOB CREWE
and BOB GAUDIO

HE'S A REBEL

Moderately, with a beat

Words and Music by
GENE PITNEY

See the way he walks down the street,
When he holds my hand I'm so proud,

watch the way he shuff-les his feet,
'Cause he's not just one of the crowd,

Oh, how he holds his head high when
My ba-by's al-ways the one to

he goes walk-in' by _____ He's my guy! _____

RUBY BABY

Words and Music by JERRY LEIBER
and MIKE STOLLER

SURFIN' U.S.A.

Music by CHUCK BERRY
Lyric by BRIAN WILSON

PIPELINE

By BOB SPICKARD
and BRIAN CARMEN

IT'S MY PARTY

Words and Music by HERB WIENER, WALLY GOLD and JOHN GLUCK, JR.

Moderately bright

No - bod - y knows____ where my John - ny has gone,____ But
Play all my rec - ords, keep danc - ing all night,____ But
Ju - dy and John - ny just walked thru the door,____

Ju - dy left____ the same time.
leave me a - lone____ for a while,
Like a queen____ with her king,

Why was he
'Til John - ny's
Oh, what a

WIPE OUT

By THE SURFARIS

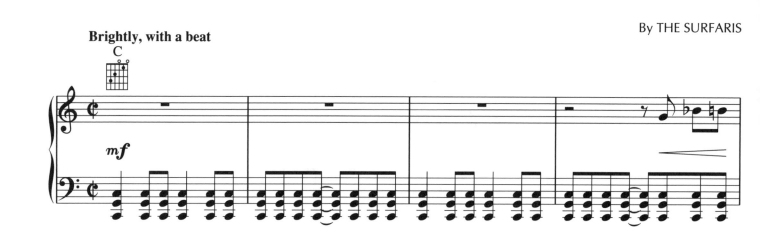

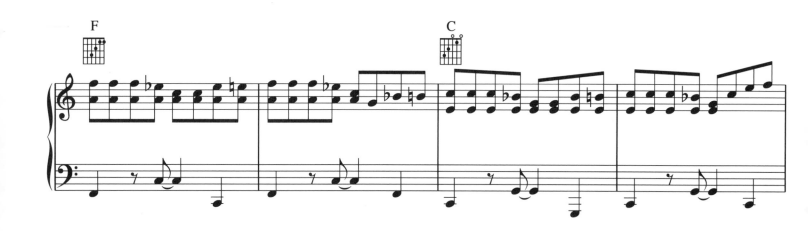

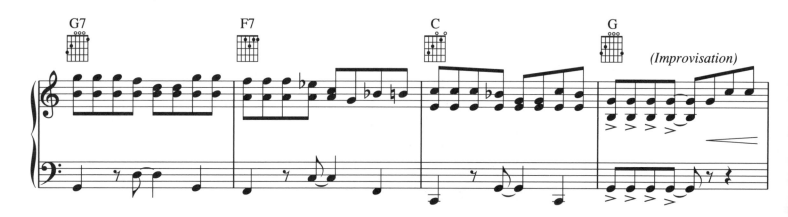

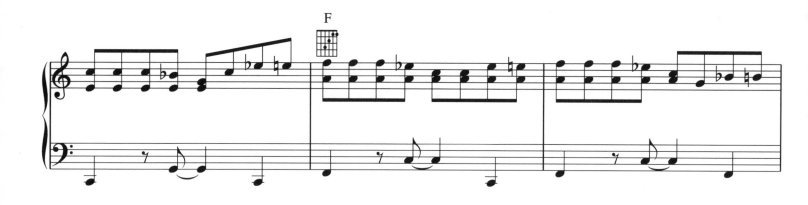

SURF CITY

Words and Music by BRIAN WILSON
and JAN BERRY

Two girls _ for ev-'ry boy! _

1. I bought a thir-ty-four wag-on and we call it a wood-y.
nev-er roll the streets up 'cause there's al-ways some-thing go-ing.
wood-y breaks down on me some-where on my surf _ route,

Surf Cit-y here we come!
You know it's not ver-y cher-ry as an
They're eith-er out surf-in' or they
I'll strap my board to my back and hitch a

BLUE VELVET

Words and Music by BERNIE WAYNE
and LEE MORRIS

SURFER GIRL

Words and Music by
BRIAN WILSON

LOUIE, LOUIE

Words and Music by
RICHARD BERRY

SUGAR SHACK

Words and Music by KEITH McCORMACK
and FAYE VOSS

GOIN' OUT OF MY HEAD

Words and Music by TEDDY RANDAZZO
and BOBBY WEINSTEIN

NADINE

By CHUCK BERRY

Very steady beat

G7

G

As I got on a cit - y bus and
saw her from the cor - ner as she

found a va - cant seat. I thought I saw my fu - ture bride___
turned and dou - bled back. She start - ed walk - in' t'ward a cof - fee

C9

walk - in' up the street I shout - ed to the driv - er, "Hey con -
col - oured Ca - di - lac. I was push - in' thru the crowd, try - in' to

Additional Lyrics

3. Down-town searchin' for her, lookin' all around,
Saw her gettin' in a yellow cab headin' up-town.
I caught a loaded taxi, paid up ev'rybody's tab
With a twenty dollar bill, told him "Catch that yellow cab".

4. She moves around like a wave of summer breeze,
Go, driver, go, go, catch her balmy breeze.
Movin' thru the traffic like a mounted cavalier.
Leanin' out the taxi window tryin' to make her hear.

HI-HEEL SNEAKERS

Words and Music by ROBERT HIGGENBOTHAM

RONNIE

Words and Music by BOB CREWE
and BOB GAUDIO

149

CHAPEL OF LOVE

Words and Music by PHIL SPECTOR,
ELLIE GREENWICH and JEFF BARRY

* Repeat from * to * for fade-out ending

NO PARTICULAR PLACE TO GO

Words and Music by
CHUCK BERRY

RAG DOLL

Words and Music by BOB CREWE
and BOB GAUDIO

UNDER THE BOARDWALK

Words and Music by
ARTIE RESNICK & KENNY YOUNG

board - walk) We'll be hav - in' some fun ____ (Un - der the

board - walk) Peo - ple walk - in' a - bove ____ (Un - der the

board - walk) we'll be fall - in' in love ____ Un - der the (un - der the

board - walk, board - walk. From the walk.
board - walk, board - walk. *Instrumental* walk.

mp

DO WAH DIDDY DIDDY

Words by JEFF BARRY
and ELLIE GREENWICH

There he was,___ just a walk-in' down the street, Sing-in' do wah did-dy did-dy,
fore I knew___ it he was walk-in' next to me, Sing-in' do wah did-dy did-dy,

down did-dy do; Pop-pin' his fin-gers and a shuf-fl-in' his feet, Sing-in'
down did-dy do; He took___ my hand ___ just as nat-'ral as can be, Sing-in'

do wah did-dy did-dy, down did-dy do. He looked good, (Yeah, yeah) He looked
do wah did-dy did-dy, down did-dy do. We walked on, (Yeah, yeah) To my

MY BOYFRIEND'S BACK

Words and Music by ROBERT (BOB) FELDMAN,
GERALD (JERRY) GOLDSTEIN and RICHARD GOTTEHRER

My boy-friend's back, and you're gon-na be in trou-ble.
He's been gone for such a long time.

(Hey, la - di - la, My boy-friend's back)

When you see him com-in', bet - ter
Now he's back and

(Hey, la - di - la, My boy-friend's back)

cut on the dou - ble.
things will be fine.

You're

LEADER OF THE PACK

Words and Music by GEORGE MORTON,
JEFF BARRY and ELLIE GREENWICH

MOUNTAIN OF LOVE

Moderately Slow

Words and Music by HAROLD DORMAN

THE BIRDS AND THE BEES

Words and Music by
HERB NEWMAN

Let me tell ya 'bout the birds and the bees and the flow-ers and the trees and the

moon up a-bove and a thing_ called love _____

Let me tell ya 'bout the stars in the sky and a girl and a guy and the

176

JOLLY GREEN GIANT

"Hey, Jolly Green Giant, What's new besides Ho! Ho! Ho!"
Would you believe a row boat with three leaky worms?

Words and Music by DON HARRIS,
DEWY TERRY JR., and LYNN EASTON

WOOLY BULLY

Words and Music by
DOMINGO SAMUDIO

Bul - ly

Additional Lyrics

2. Hatty told Matty
   Let's don't take no chance,
   Let's not be L 7
   Come and learn to dance
   Wooly bully — wooly bully —
   Wooly bully — wooly bully — wooly bully.

3 Matty told Hatty
   That's the thing to do,
   Get yo' someone really
   To pull the wool with you —
   Wooly bully — wooly bully
   Wooly bully — wooly bully — wooly bully.

The most definitive set of rock songbooks ever published! Each book contains over 30 big hits arranged for piano, voice and guitar, as well as a detailed rock history of the times – complete with photos and chart records of the songs. Every rock historian and fan will want to make this series part of their collection!

BIRTH OF ROCK AND ROLL

This first volume explores rock's rhythm and blues roots and its earliest tunes – from "Rocket '88" and "Shake, Rattle And Roll" to the major hits of Elvis Presley, Little Richard, Jerry Lee Lewis, Buddy Holly, and more.

Song highlights include: All Shook Up • Blueberry Hill • Blue Suede Shoes • Earth Angel • Heartbreak Hotel • Long Tall Sally • Lucille • Goodnight, It's Time To Go • The Green Door • Rock Around The Clock • Tutti-Frutti • and more! 00490216/$12.95

THE HISTORY OF ROCK
THE DEFINITIVE ROCK & ROLL SERIES

THE LATE '50S

The declaration "Rock And Roll Is Here To Stay" led the way for American Bandstand greats like Paul Anka, Frankie Avalon, Fabian, Bobby Darin, and Connie Francis. This book also explores the novelty song hits, the close harmony styles, and romantic ballads that filled the radio waves.

Song highlights include: At The Hop • Chantilly Lace • Do You Want To Dance? • Great Balls Of Fire • Lollipop • Rock And Roll Is Here To Stay • Sea Of Love • Splish Splash • Tears On My Pillow • Tequila • Wake Up, Little Susie • Yakety Yak • and more. 00490321/$14.95

For more information see your local music dealer or contact:

Hal Leonard Publishing Corporation
7777 West Bluemound Road P.O. Box 13819 Milwaukee, WI 53213

Prices, availability and contents subject to change without notice

THE EARLY '60S

Surf music, doo wop, and dance crazes set the stage for a new decade. This volume explores the success of the Beach Boys, "Big Girls Don't Cry," and the Twist.

Song highlights include: Barbara Ann • Breaking Up Is Hard To Do • Do Wah Diddy Diddy • Duke Of Earl • Hit The Road, Jack • Louie, Louie • My Boyfriend's Back • Runaway • Sherry • Surfin' U.S.A. • Tell Laura I Love Her • The Twist • Under The Boardwalk • Wooly Bully • and more.
00490322/$14.95

THE MID '60S

The British invaded the charts and Hendrix re-invented the guitar in this volume, featuring chart toppers of the Beatles, the Moody Blues, the Hollies, Rolling Stones, Mamas and Papas, James Brown, the Byrds, and many more.

Song highlights include: All Day And All Of The Night • California Dreamin' • Can't Buy Me Love • Dedicated To The One I Love • For Your Love • Gloria • Groovin' • Help! • Hey Joe • I Want To Hold Your Hand • Papa's Got A Brand New Bag • Summer In The City • Wild Thing • Yesterday • and more.
00490581/$14.95

THE LATE '60S

The turbulence of this era created a new mood for rock and roll. From the classic "Sgt. Pepper's Lonely Hearts Club Band" to the San Francisco sound to Janis Joplin to the jazz/rock hits of Blood, Sweat and Tears, you'll find the songs that made the statements of the time in this volume.

Song highlights: Abraham, Martin And John • And When I Die • Born To Be Wild • Come Together • Hey Jude • Incense And Peppermints • The Letter • The Magic Bus • San Francisco (Be Sure To Some Wear Flowers In Your Hair) • Spinning Wheel • The Sunshine Of Your Love • White Room • A Whiter Shade Of Pale.
00311505/$12.95